ONLINE TEACHING TOOLBOX

BEST PRACTICES, STRATEGIES, AND ACTIVITIES FOR EFFECTIVE ONLINE TEACHING

LORIE A. SOUSA PHD

CONTENTS

Preface

Students often ask, "Why do I need to know this?" You may be asking yourself that same question about online instruction. Many of you may have been thrust into it against your will "virtually" overnight and may be reluctant participants in this global experiment. This book is intended for the beginner and perhaps reluctant online instructor. If is focused primarily on social science in the domain of higher education but many of the ideas and tools could be adapted for use in secondary education and other domains as well. My intention in writing this book is to share my enthusiasm for online instruction based on my experience as an educational researcher (since 2001) and online instructor (since 2013) with multiple national and international universities. I hope that the information I have accumulated through trainings, reading the academic literature, and many years of online teaching experience will be helpful to you. Throughout this book I will share best practices, ideas for activities and assignments, provide a bit of research from the literature, and tools to investigate that will increase efficiency, effectiveness, and enjoyment in the online classroom.

Whether face-to-face (f2f) or online, the goal is to provide quality instruction. Instead of looking at online instruction as a poor substitute for f2f instruction (which the research suggests is not the case; more on that later), we *could* try to celebrate change and adapt by finding ways to do things we could not do (or could not do as easily) in a f2f classroom and enhance our instruction by embracing the differences.

1

FOUNDATION - INTRODUCTION

Online education is here to stay so we may as well get good at it. A global health crisis may have been your introduction into the world of online instruction, but there are many other reasons educational institutions may choose to offer more and more of their course catalog online. Lack of space to expand facilities as well as the funds necessary to build new facilities will likely encourage institutions to offer more courses online. Budget is also another consideration. More students can be accommodated by providing course offerings online which tends to be more cost effective. Online courses also allow institutions to expand their enrollment to non-traditional and foreign students.

Those of you who thrive off the f2f environment may be skeptical about whether you can be as effective in an online classroom. Whether you intend to teach online temporarily or permanently, I hope that by the time you finish this book you will have an appreciation for some of the amazing things you can achieve in an online classroom.

Today's students are comfortable with screens and technology. It is up to us to catch up and learn the best methods to ensure that the technology accelerates and enhances learning rather than serving as an unwieldy obstacle.

This book is:

- geared more toward institutions of higher learning, as that is where I gained most of my teaching experience. However, the chapters on activities and tools may be relevant for secondary instruction as well.

- intended to be a brief beginner guide rather than a comprehensive review of the literature, thus, I have focused more on the practical aspects of online education rather than doing a deep dive into the distance learning literature, though I have tried to provide references to academic sources and a brief bibliography in Chapter 7 for those who want to investigate further.

Advantages of Online Instruction

For those still skeptical about the advantages of online instruction, I offer seven macro level and seven micro level reasons that online instruction can be advantageous to teachers, students, institutions, and the learning process.

7 Macro Advantages

1. <u>Equity</u>: Many students do not have the time and resources necessary to attend traditional institutions of higher learning. Some students from lower income households must work full-time or they may have to care for family members, which does not allow them the freedom to adhere to a traditional schedule. I have also had many students with chronic physical and mental health issues such as Lupus and Rheumatoid Arthritis or Anxiety and Depression, who were better accommodated by the flexibility of online instruction during flares or during periods where they have many doctors' appointments. Online education has the potential to address some of the economic and physical/mental health inequities that are more difficult to address with a traditional educational model.

2. <u>Facilities</u>: Online courses offer learning opportunities to students who might not be accommodated at an institution

due to lack of space or the financial resources necessary to expand. Online offerings can help provide expanded course work that eases impacted majors and may even help students complete their requirements in a timely manner rather than enduring the frustrations of limited course selection and delayed graduations due to highly impacted courses.

3. <u>Reach</u>: Online courses allow institutions to reach students who they might otherwise not be able to enroll due to geographical considerations.

4. <u>Fiscal</u>: Fiscal considerations are becoming increasingly important to educational institutions. Online courses can allow for increased enrollment with less use of resources. As administrators, teachers, and students become more comfortable with online instruction, the expectation is that the economic benefits will encourage expansion of online course offerings.

5. <u>Anxious/Introverted students</u>: As teachers we have all done our best to assist students with anxious and introverted personalities, like the shy student who never says a word in class or the academic perfectionist who won't share their thoughts because they are too afraid to make a mistake in public. The world is really built for extroverts. The online environment can be a more comfortable place for introverts. I found in my f2f classes that the same 5-8 people were carrying 80% of the discussion. As much as I would prompt and try to include other students, I often got worn out and relied on a few students to speak for the class. I have found in my online discussions, that many students who felt uncomfortable speaking up in class were the biggest contributors to the online discussions. The "virtual" anonymity seemed to help diminish their fears in a wonderful way. Student feedback suggests that online discussions were often student's favorite parts of my courses.

Online forums introduced a democratization that was unexpected and a delightful side effect.

6. <u>In Real Life (IRL)</u>: The online environment will more closely mimic the working world that students will find themselves in after graduation. Face-to-face interaction will never go out of favor, and the f2f interactions students experience in school are very valuable. Online courses will more closely align with their experiences in a professional environment which will likely require them to research and leverage resources to complete projects using various technologies and to communicate effectively in written form. Students certainly have plenty of screen time via social media and texting, but this is very different from a professional environment where they will be expected to write in full sentences and communicate their ideas effectively using the latest technology. In addition, as remote work becomes more and more accepted and desirable to both employees and employers, many of our students may eventually work on teams with members scattered around the world. Skills obtained in online classroom environments may give students an advantage post-graduation in professional environments. This is not to say that these things can't be taught in a f2f classroom. They certainly can. But online courses *require* the use of technology in every respect and thus may naturally lend itself toward adoption of these skills.

7. <u>Environmentally Friendly</u>: In online learning there is less use of paper and resources such as energy and other utilities. There is also less use of transportation, which helps reduce greenhouse gases. One study found that online courses consume 90% less energy (Roy et. al., 2005). Online courses can also result in 85% less CO_2 emissions per student than traditional in-person courses.

7 Micro Advantages

1. <u>Muli-media</u>: Learning that is conducted online is uniquely positioned to encourage the use of technological resources in all of their many forms. When preparing a learning unit or module, videos, podcasts, data, or links to source materials can be easily and simply made available to learners to supplement lecture or text.

2. <u>Pacing</u>: Differentiated instruction is a necessary yet complicated part of teaching. Classrooms almost always contain a variety of ability levels. Teachers spend much of their time making sure that advanced students aren't bored, and beginners aren't left behind. Online platforms allow for self-pacing that is difficult to achieve in a f2f classroom. Students who are struggling can take in the lectures at their own pace, slowing down to revisit complex concepts, pausing to look something up that is unfamiliar or unclear, while advanced students can venture ahead. This is especially true in courses with asynchronous content.

3. <u>Speed</u>: Students in my courses have reported speeding up or slowing down the speed of the recorded lectures depending on their comfort level with the content. A student who is comfortable with the concepts or has a prior foundation can speed up the lecture to double time which can help reduce boredom and retain their interest. Meanwhile, another student struggling with the same content can slow it down to half speed to provide more space to process the information which reduces frustration and likelihood of shutting down or withdrawing from it.

4. <u>Flexibility</u>: The flexibility of online learning is a benefit to both teachers and students. I have had students who have to work full-time or have children, siblings, parents, or grandparents that they have caregiving responsibilities for while attending school. The opportunity to continue their education could mean the difference between remaining in

poverty and the ability to improve their life circumstances. Not all students have the privilege of focusing solely on school and those who don't, need educational opportunities all the more.

5. <u>Wait time</u>: This is another advantage that is inherent to online asynchronous learning. Giving students time to marinate in the content can be difficult to achieve in f2f environments when there is so much to cover and so little time. When students can ask questions on the spot, it can inhibit their ability to think through the problem themselves and experience the struggle that is so necessary for learning of difficult concepts. I have had students who watched one of my lectures and emailed immediately with a question, only to email again later the same day before I could get back to them letting me know that they figured it out on their own. This is a valuable part of the learning process that is built right into the asynchronous online learning structure.

6. <u>Recorded/Recordable Lectures</u>: This is an advantage of both synchronous and asynchronous online formats. Lectures that are initially recorded or are recordable can be provided to absent students. As mentioned previously, lectures can also be replayed, slowed down, paused, or revisited by students who might be struggling with the material or want to review before an exam. Lectures can be embedded with questions throughout using tools like Playposit to check for understanding. More information about Playposit can be found in Chapter 5. Encouraging engagement with lectures will be addressed in Chapter 2.

7. <u>Quicker and more extensive feedback</u>: Extensive and timely feedback has been linked to improved performance and self-efficacy (Karl et. al., 1993). Online quizzes and tests allow for immediate feedback on score and incorrect responses. Instructors are also more easily able to provide extensive feedback on assignments and papers by tying feedback to

digital rubrics, use of templates, and embedding links to examples and additional resources.

Please consider this book an ala carte menu of ideas and strategies. It is important to remember that you don't have to do it all. Too much technology can overwhelm both teacher and student. As with all toolboxes, the key is to find the tool that works best for the job.

2

NUTS & BOLTS - BEST PRACTICES

There are a number of best practices that I have found to be helpful as I have revised my courses over the years to improve communication with students and be very explicit about what I am asking them to do and when they need to do it. Not all suggestions I make in this chapter are specific to online learning but are perhaps even more crucial in the online format to clearly communicate expectations, reduce frustration, encourage interaction with the online community, and engagement with the materials.

Blueprints: Organization, Consistency, & Clarity

- **Simplicity** is essential. Students will be overwhelmed if messaging, instructions, or the technologies they are required to interact with are overcomplicated.
- Send out **weekly reminders** on Sundays or Mondays with all due dates for the week
- Send reminder emails on Big Days (e.g. Midterm, Paper, Finals, Project due dates)

EXAMPLE:

Hello Class,

You are responsible for the following this week:

1. Read Chapters 11 and 14.
2. If you haven't already completed your 2 hours of experimental credit for the department, you must do so before the final exam.
3. Work on proofing and finalizing your Research Proposal.
4. Turn in your Research Proposal by Wed.
5. Study for Final.

Note about the Research Proposal: Please make sure that you proof your papers thoroughly and have at least one other person (preferably 2) proof your paper before you turn it in. If you don't have anyone to proof-read for you, use text-to-speech software to hear your paper spoken aloud to you. Many errors can be heard when overlooked at a reading. Follow the rubric closely and make sure you submit ALL required sections. Points will be taken off for improper APA format and incorrect grammar/spelling and typos. Make sure you submit a "clean and polished" academic paper. If you are unsure of what is included or how to apply APA format, refer to the sample paper I have provided in the Writing Resources tab and/or your APA Manual. Your textbook Appendix A is also an excellent resource. I have provided you with MULTIPLE resources including an audio PPT, rubric, sample paper, detailed instructions, and APA Manual Example, so you should have everything you need to write a solid Research Proposal.

Good luck,

Dr. S

- Be **consistent with messaging** and assignments. Have the announcements go out on the same day each week. Have weekly assignments due on the same day of the week. Set up an expectation to provide the structure and framework that helps students stay on track. For example, I have initial discussion posts due on Wednesdays and student replies to their peers by Sunday of each week. The consistency helps students stay on track and anticipate their deadlines.
- Be **clear and concise** in language. Excessively long communications with unnecessary information will be ignored.
- **Repetition** is vital in an online environment. You may have to repeat important messages in multiple formats, multiple times. For instance, I provide the information for tutoring services in every announcement that I send out. I have found if it is only mentioned once or twice, students will miss it.
- Have a file with **lists of resources** including phone numbers and email addresses for tutoring, writing center, help desk for technical issues, or library services, etc. that you can easily copy and paste into responses to student emails.
- A **comprehensive syllabus** is essential. Make sure the syllabus is solid and include easy to read matrices (See example in Appendix).
- It can be helpful to provide a **Syllabus quiz** for extra credit to encourage students to read it (See example in Appendix).
- Utilize **formative and summative assessment.** Formative assessment results should be provided to students immediately if possible so that they can identify areas they need to focus on, and course correct. Summative assessments will be the bulk of the student's grades.
- Provide a list of **learning objectives** for each unit. A list of objectives will guide your instructional design and make sure there is good alignment throughout the course. It is also helpful to students to frame the learning, identify expectations, and to use as a study guide for exams.

- **Captioning** of any videos you record or make available to students is especially helpful for students with learning disabilities, physical disabilities, or students for whom English is a second language. Most video recording applications will have a captioning feature. I was able to take audio PowerPoints that I created and convert them to video on YouTube, which did a very good job of automatically captioning my recording. It is important to speak clearly and annunciate for artificial intelligence to accurately caption your words. If, however, there is any issue with the video making it unintelligible in areas, YouTube also allows you to edit and correct any words that were captioned incorrectly.

- Keep concepts of **Universal Design for Learning** (UDL) in mind to maintain access for students with diverse abilities. Universal design principles are applied to insure equal access to materials for all. There are recommendations for resources in Chapter 6 that can help you meet UDL guidelines.

- **Providing content in multiple ways** can increase the usefulness of your lessons. I provide my lectures in both printable slide format for downloading of hard copies and video that allows for streaming and captioning.

- **Provide detailed instructions** so that expectations are clearly communicated. I have found that also providing verbal instructions in video form in addition to written instructions as well as rubrics and sample papers are especially important for students to understand your expectations.

- Provide **detailed feedback** often so that students are very clear on areas needing improvement. In an online class this takes on an added importance. In an asynchronous course, feedback is one of your only ways to provide direct instruction.

- Scripts can be used to increase efficiency for common errors

EXAMPLE

Hello Felicity,

I really appreciate the effort that you put into this paper.

Good job on the title page, though the running header needed to be all caps.

The content of the abstract was good, though it could have been written more precisely. The language was a bit casual in spots and a bit vague. There needed to be more citations early in the paper. Content of the lit review was good though you referred to articles as journals throughout. The articles are the individual pieces of writing included in the journals. Journals consist of multiple articles written by different authors.

The instructions, rubric, sample paper, and my emails on the topic discussed the various sections you were to include in your paper. Unfortunately, you didn't delineate the sections, so I am unclear on whether there was an Aims section and what was included in your Methods. The area that seemed to discuss Methods also did not have the level of detail needed for a proposal of this kind.

Toward the end you discuss proving your hypothesis. As researchers we don't seek to prove our hypothesis. We seek to test it. We can't root for finding one result over another as it is really important to remain impartial as scientists.

References were not in APA Style. They must be from peer reviewed Psychology Journals. Never from blogs, magazines, or newspapers. It is very important that your sources are valid.

Writing needed some additional polishing and more of a scholarly and academic tone. It was a bit casual in some places.

There were some grammatical issues that impacted clarity and understanding. My recommendation on papers is to have someone read and proof it for you before submission. Preferably someone unfamiliar with the content. If that is not possible, there are great free text to speech software programs online that will read your paper aloud so you can hear if there are any sentence structure, grammar, or spelling issues.

Dr. S

- Create a **feedback library**. With projects and papers, there are often common mistakes that you see again and again. Because the feedback is electronic, you are able to copy and paste in guidance on common errors. I add to my feedback libraries regularly. This is an advantage in the online setting as all assignments will be electronic, allowing for much more detailed feedback for common mistakes. Of course, it is important to customize the feedback as much as possible, but if you see the same citation method error again and again, it makes sense to write some well worded guidance and pop it into the feedback among your other more personalized statements about their work.
- Create a **Frequently Asked Questions** (FAQ) section in your discussion forums to address issues that come up every term. It will save you time in the long run because you won't have to answer the same questions via email multiple times.
- Create **Class Level Questions Discussion Forums.** Many instructors find this kind of thing very helpful. Students can ask each other for their understanding of things or clarification without having to contact the instructor. I have found that this is useful depending on the course. I once taught a course with a very unique format. It was so different from other courses that students were always confused and anxious about it. In this course the questions posed in the forum were often answered incorrectly by other students

which created even more confusion and anxiety. In this particular case I chose to eliminate this forum. However, when I received questions from students that I felt were useful to the entire class, I would send out an email and post an announcement so all students would receive a consistent message.

- **Scaffolding** of assignments is a useful tool to help students ease into large projects or papers. It is especially helpful when the process is entirely new to them. In my Research Methods course students are required to complete a research proposal by the end of the term. For some students this is the first time they have been asked to write a technical paper. Up until this point they have only participated in creative writing or persuasive writing. Research papers are an entirely different thing and the rules for a paper of this kind are vastly different. I try to break things up into smaller more manageable tasks. With a scaffolded assignment they get feedback along the way so that they can course correct in time for their final draft submission.

EXAMPLE

Scaffolded Assignment
Final Deliverable: *APA Style Research Proposal*
Methods and Research in Psychology

Week Due	Assignment Piece	Points (30% of overall grade)
Week 3	Submit Topic	5
Week 5	Submit Abstract	10
Week 8	Submit Lit Review	20
Week 10	Submit Aims & Methods	25
Week 12	Submit Draft for Peer Review*	10
Week 14	Submit Peer Review of Partner's Proposal	30
Week 15	Submit Final Draft (Revised based upon feedback)	100

*If your partner does not get a draft to you by the deadline, please reach out to me and let me know. I can send you a draft so that you are able to complete the assignment.
**Late submissions will be graded but no feedback will be provided unless prior arrangements have been made with me ahead of time, thus, it will benefit your final score to submit all assignments on time.

- Online courses can either be **Synchronous, Asynchronous, or a hybrid of both.** Each have pros and cons. The primary advantage with Synchronous is that it is familiar. It is the method that most students and instructors are comfortable with because it most closely mimics the f2f classroom. I believe this advantage will decrease over time as online instruction becomes ubiquitous. I have covered many of the advantages of Asynchronous learning in chapter one including that it most closely mimics the workplace, pacing, and flexibility. Non-traditional students are best served asynchronously due to their schedules and responsibilities.
- **Recorded lectures** should be no more than 30 mins or preferably 3, 10 min videos to retain attention.
- Allow for **technical issues.** The online element can introduce a bit of unpredictability. I have found it is best to give students the benefit of the doubt unless it becomes excessive. There are so many factors that can cause technical issues from bandwidth problems, Wi-Fi issues, and overloaded systems, to firewalls and browser incompatibilities. Reassure students that you are sympathetic to their issues and always have the school's tech support number and email on hand to refer students to assistance.

Building Community: Participation & Engagement

- I require students record a **biographical video** and post it in the first discussion forum. I find it is a great community builder and helps students bond a bit as the course begins. I provide an instructional video on how they can do this. I also record a video of my own to introduce me to the class and give them some insight into my teaching philosophy and background at the top of the course. It helps students to connect with me and their peers and sets a good tone.

- Provide a video taking students through the Learning Management System, highlighting areas of importance. Also provide contact information for your school's tech support so they can receive assistance and reduce frustration.
- Responsiveness is so crucial in an online class. In a f2f class, a student knows that they can ask you questions in class and when they will get their answers (during scheduled class time). In an online class, lack of responsiveness can lead to students feeling adrift and unsupported. It also doesn't allow them to plan or progress in their work. The rule of thumb is to always **respond within 24 hours.** Write this rule into the syllabus and let them know from the outset that if they don't hear from you in 24 hours they should try another method of contacting you. Sometimes emails don't arrive or cell numbers are incorrectly entered so it is good to let them know you always follow this rule and that if they don't hear from you it isn't neglect, it could be a technical issue.
- **Peer review** assignments are a great way to encourage community in addition to being a great teaching tool. It is pretty universally accepted that the best way to learn something is to teach it. It forces students to compare the work product to a rubric which in turn gives them more insight into what they need to do to improve their own work. It also gets them to engage with the material multiple times which benefits comprehension and retention.
- Assignments must be **personally relevant and current (as much as possible)** and should be revised and updated often. At the beginning of the COVID-19 pandemic I was teaching Human Development. There were only a few discussion opportunities left in the semester. It felt wrong to ignore something so monumental that was happening on such a global scale. I wanted to find a way to give students an opportunity to share their experiences in a way that was relevant to the course. The result was beyond my

expectations. Students wrote more on this topic than any other and in the evaluations, students wrote that it was a bonding experience that brought students together.

- EXAMPLE

Discussion #13

We are currently living through something historic and there is no point in pretending that we won't be changed by this experience. Historical effects can impact how we see the world and who we are, sometimes without our awareness.

This week you have been learning about memory and it got me thinking about how our memories help us create a narrative for our lives that influences what we think of ourselves and helps to form our identities. For example, my grandfather lost his entire family in the 1918 influenza pandemic when he was a child and ended up in an orphanage. His story of resiliency, independence, and hard work influenced my father and was passed down to me and now to my daughter. With your memories and personal narrative in mind, answer the following questions:

1. What memories do you think you will have from this time? (2 extra points for referencing your textbook in your discussion of memory)

2. How do you think living through this time in our history will influence your personal narrative?

3. When you are 70 years old, what will you be telling youngsters about this time?

4. Share something that is making you happy right now. It could be a new band you found, crafting, spending time with your family, a game, a video, a recipe, a Tik Tok, anything that is getting you through that you want to share with your classmates. Please attach a link to your response if possible.

I hope everyone is healthy and thriving despite everything going on.

*If you would like to do an alternate assignment in place of this assignment, please email me and let me know.

- **Check in** with students individually at least twice per term. This personal touch goes a long way with students. Students in online courses can feel isolated from their instructors and their peers. Sending out a couple of quick check-ins per term can make a big difference in their level of engagement.
- **Embed multi-media** into your course. Podcasts and videos are a great way to increase engagement and introduce students to different perspectives.
- Conduct **class surveys** to learn more about your students. I will ask questions about whether they work, whether they have any background in the course, or interest in the subject matter, for example. I have done this in several of my courses and find that it helps me get to know my students. Survey software such as Survey Monkey, Alchemist (formerly Survey Gizmo), and Google Forms are very user friendly and easy to deploy. More on that in Chapter 5.
- A **Warm and engaging style** goes a long way to ease issues related to the impersonal nature of online communication. Some general rules of thumb include:
- Always address the person by name.
- Share a personal story (not too personal).
- Demonstrate empathy by expressing understanding for their concerns and hardships.
- Reassure them that you are there to support them and provide assistance.
- Refer them out to additional resources such as library services, writing center, tutoring, help desk for technology issues, etc. when additional help is needed so they know there is a team of people ready to support them.
- Send them links to online resources such as tutorials or sites with helpful information.

- Always end emails with, "Please let me know if you have any other questions or require additional assistance or support."

3

BUILDING BLOCKS – INSTRUCTIONAL DESIGN ELEMENTS

When building a new course, I always begin with sketching out an outline of the elements I want to include. Instructional design is intentional and involves careful planning and organization with an awareness of research in the domains of learning, brain science, usability and motivation. The guiding principles from the research incorporated into my suggestions include elements that are intended to consider engagement, motivation, cognition, behavior, and executive brain function.

The content to follow are some basic building blocks that are useful to consider when starting to craft a course from scratch. I don't always deploy every single one of these elements for every course I teach, but you would find some combination of most of them throughout my courses.

Learning Objectives: I generally begin curriculum development by constructing the learning objectives. They provide a useful guide for the entire course and are a great tool to make sure that all units are aligned with what you want students to learn over the course of the term. They also serve as a check on the final course content to ensure I have enough coverage for each of the objectives.

Quizzes: Weekly quizzes provide a valuable formative assessment piece. I generally allow students to receive their results as soon as they complete their quiz so that they know which areas they are having difficulty with immediately and can use that information to ask questions or seek out understanding in their text or online tutorials.

Discussions: Weekly or biweekly discussions serve multiple functions. They encourage interaction with peers which helps to create a sense of community that can be lost in an online course. But, most importantly, they provide students with an opportunity to process and engage with the course content in a way that they might not be able to otherwise. There is a depth of understanding that occurs when students are asked to answer questions and apply their knowledge of the materials. Discussions are one of the greatest strengths of an online course. In online courses, students are all required to contribute, there is no limit to how much they can write, and no time constraints. Students in my courses say that the discussions were the most valuable part of the class.

Assignments: Depending on the course, I will sometimes create assignments that target a particular concept that I have seen students struggle with in the past so that they get some practice. For example, students often have difficulty with identifying independent and dependent variables when they are reading articles in the psychology literature. Because of this, I developed a brief assignment to provide students with some direct exposure to the concepts. They had to find an article that they were interested in from a peer reviewed psychology journal and then provide a summary of the article and identify the sample, research questions, independent and dependent variables as well as any limitations they perceived in the study. This really helped students when they had to write a research proposal of their own. I immediately saw an increase in the quality of their final papers after I inserted this assignment into the curriculum. Sometimes students don't know what they don't know until they have to perform a task related to their understanding of the concepts.

Projects or Project Based Learning: There is a great deal of research demonstrating the benefits of projects and project-based learning (PBL) that educators reading this book will be well aware of. Projects tend to lead to deeper understanding of concepts and higher levels of engagement. With project-based learning, the levels of learning are even deeper and longer lasting. It can also encourage the development of independent learning or group collaboration skills depending on the type of project assigned. Projects are also valuable by more closely mimicking the real-world work environment.

Papers: Papers can be an essential tool to increase learning of complex concepts that cannot be explored as easily using other methods. It gives students opportunities to take a deep dive into a topic. While other forms of evaluation in the classroom may assess rote memorization, papers require students to use many of the skills they will need after college in their careers including, conducting research, reading comprehension, critical thinking, analysis, evaluation of credible resources, application of academic writing standards (APA Style, MLA, Chicago Style), differentiation between technical vs. persuasive vs. narrative forms of writing, and grammar and spelling.

Presentations: Much like projects and papers, preparing and delivering presentations provide another avenue toward learning, a way to evaluate understanding, and is a tool useful for most careers. Presentation skills are also valuable in the interview process. With so many meetings and events going online during the pandemic, comfort level in front of the camera is likely to be an essential skill in the future.

Exams: Midterms and final exams are staples of student assessment. They may be multiple choice, short answer, or essay. I generally try to provide a midterm to give students some feedback on how they are performing midway through the term. It is an opportunity for formative assessment. Students sometimes think they know more than they do. A midterm is a great way to give them some feedback regarding their general knowledge in the course. It often serves as a wake-up call and gives students an idea of where they need to shore things up so they can do better on the final exam. Final exams are the summative assessment portion of the assessment library. It will be your students' last opportunity to demonstrate what they have learned. I try to make my final exams cumulative with both multiple choice and essay/short answer questions in an effort to give them more opportunities to succeed. I tend to allow open-book but with a limited time frame to complete the exam.

Syllabus: I believe it is best to make the syllabus as explicit as possible. A good syllabus is organized, detailed, and includes a calendar which shows exactly when everything is due. It also includes information on course policies, course learning objectives, numbers and links to resources, and clear communication of expectations. I continually revise my syllabus as students ask questions or communicate that something has been unclear to them. I also always provide an extra credit opportunity for students with a syllabus quiz. Students must read the entire syllabus to do well on the syllabus quiz. Examples of a course syllabus and syllabus quiz are in the Appendix.

Multi-Media: Online learning increases access to wonderful multi-media opportunities that can enhance and accelerate learning. Students often have preferences for different methods of receiving information. When designing your online course, it is much simpler to embed content to present ideas in multiple ways vs. in a traditional classroom. For example, in addition to assigning reading from the text and providing a lecture on the chapter, I will also identify concepts that appear to be most challenging for students based on the questions I get and how they have performed on exams. I will then seek out resources that might help students better understand the concept including podcasts, YouTube videos, Kahn Academy videos, and links to websites with relevant information.

Peer Review: I sometimes assign peer review tasks primarily because I noticed that students were not reading through the instructions on papers and assignments in their entirety. They would leave out entire sections or demonstrate in other ways that they had clearly not read through the materials. Seneca, a Roman philosopher said, "While we teach, we learn." By requiring students to review another student's work, they must read the instructions to see what is required and consult a rubric to grade and provide feedback to their classmate.

Scaffolding: By taking a more complicated assignment, project, or paper and splitting it into several steps, each of which is turned in for feedback, students have the opportunity to progress in their learning as they process the feedback and apply it, building toward the final submission.

4

FLOOR PLAN – 60 ACTIVITIES & ASSIGNMENTS

This chapter is intended to provide some ideas for fun activities that lend themselves to online learning. Depending on your instructional area, some of these suggestions may be more or less relevant. The purpose in providing suggested activities and assignments is to help start the creative process and inspire ideas that can help increase engagement. I tried to include activities and assignments that could apply to multiple subject matter areas or could be converted to fit multiple domains. Thus, many of the suggestions are more generic but could be modified to fit your content area.

1. "Easter egg" assignments.

Hide Easter eggs assignments in video content to encourage viewing. Students must watch or listen to recorded lectures to receive instructions on quick assignments that are hidden like Easter eggs throughout the lectures. Assignments could be creating a chart with important concepts or creating a multiple-choice question on the concept discussed in the video. I generally make these assignments extra credit. Then at the end of the term when students are asking for extra credit, I remind them that there are extra credit opportunities in the lectures and reviewing the lectures before the final would be a good use of their time anyways.

2. TikTok.

Have students create a brief informational TikTok to share with the class on a relevant topic.

3. Current Event Discussion Prompt.

Create discussion prompts that are relevant to current events. Have students present links to the current event and how it relates back to the topic or concepts you are working on in class.

4. Vlog.

Have students create a video or vlog to demonstrate understanding of a concept. Assign a different concept to each student. Then have students respond to a classmate and share what they have learned.

5. Multiple Choice Questions.

Students generate multiple choice questions on a topic with rationale for wrong answers.

6. Peer Review.

Have students review and provide feedback for a fellow student's draft of their paper using the rubric you will use on their final draft. This is a great way for students to become familiar with the rubric and will likely inform their own revision before final submission.

7. Debate.

Assign a debate for either live discussion or in written forums; surnames with A-L take Pro and M-Z take Con.

8. Digital Flash Cards.

Have students create digital flash cards before an exam to share with the class. Assign different concepts or chapters to each student.

9. Critique.

Students read a journal article and provide a video or audio summary and critique including limitations and what they would have done differently to improve the rigor of the work.

10. Teacher/Student Pairs.

Assign pairs of students to work together. They must research assigned topics and teach it to their partner and then create a slide presentation about what they learned.

11. Virtual Museum.

Have students create a Virtual Museum using presentation software such as PowerPoint or Google Slides with links to artifacts and information.

12. Movie Review.

Assign a movie on a relevant topic and have students record a video review.

13. Clarification Questions.

Have students pose a question about a concept they are struggling with in the discussion forum and have other students respond.

14. Student Generated Exam Questions.

Before exams, have students try to predict what concepts will be covered on the exam by asking a question they think may appear on the exam. Other students must reply by answering the question.

15. Annotated Bibliography.

Ask students to create a bibliography or annotated references page on a given topic.

16. Field Notes.

Have students view videos or simulations which allow for an online observation and have them create field notes or lab notes based upon their observations.

17. Shark Tank.

Students develop a "Shark Tank" style pitch of competing theories and present to a class synchronously for asynchronously in an infomercial style presentation.

18. Digital Concept Mapping.

Provide students with free access to digital concept mapping software and assign a topic. Students must create a concept map and submit it for credit.

19. Draw the Week.

Have students draw a visual representation of what they have learned that week. No words, just visuals.

20. Point of View (POV).

Students must take the perspective of a historical figure, famous scientist, mathematician, psychologist, etc. (whatever is relevant to your subject) and write or present from their perspective. Extra credit for costumes.

21. Virtual Escape Room.

Create a virtual escape room with puzzles related to class topics.

22. Vocabulary Guessing Game.

Students are assignment concepts and must generate an example that illustrates the concept. Then other students must guess the term from the example provided. Could be done either written or synchronously in class (EXAMPLE; cognitive dissonance, gaslighting, attribution bias).

23. Infographic.

Ask students to create an infographic on an assigned topic. There are software programs such as Venngage or they can freestyle.

24. Teacher for a Day.

Have students apply a rubric to a sample paper and grade it before their own papers are due. Then go over the range in grades and what you will be looking for on their papers.

25. Virtual Field Trips/Tours.

Many famous places and universities have virtual tours available online. Provide students with a list of links to virtual tours and have them write up their impressions and what they learned.

26. Crossword puzzle.

Use BookWidgets to create a crossword puzzle using your vocabulary for a current unit.

27. One Minute Paper.

Set a timer and give students one minute to write down everything they know about a topic.

28. 20 Questions.

Students ask questions of the teacher that only require yes or no answers to identify the term or historical figure the teacher has secretly identified ahead of time.

29. Virtual Guest Speakers.

Online courses make it very convenient to expose students to guest speakers from around the world. Colleagues are often very amenable to sharing their expertise with your class, especially if you promise to visit their class and share your work in return.

30. Scavenger Hunt.

Create a scavenger hunt for students that encourages them to explore your own Learning Management System so that they can become more familiar with where everything can be found. They can take screenshots of things and pull them into a pdf or slides to receive credit for each found item. Scavenger hunts can also be created for other websites that you want your students to become acquainted with such as online libraries or other educational resources.

31. Tutorials.

Assign a topic or have students select a relevant topic of their choosing and have them create a tutorial video to share with the class.

32. Animations.

Introduce students to animation software and have them create a short, animated video to demonstrate their understanding of a relevant concept (EXAMPLES: diffusion of responsibility, stereotyping).

33. Quiz Show.

This activity would be best suited to a synchronous format. Prepare questions before exams and conduct a quiz show using software like Kahoot! Students will appreciate the extra study time and you will be communicating what you think they should be focused on when they study for the exam.

34. Poll/Survey.

Students create an online poll or survey, collect data, and write a brief report about what they learn.

35. Make Your Case.

Have students indicate where they stand on a topic and then have them make their case in a breakout room of students who agree and then repeat the process in a breakout room of students who don't agree. Have a discussion from both the audience and presenter perspective. Then have students watch a video describing the Dunning-Kruger Effect.

36. Empathy Mapping.

Assign students a character from literature, a product user, a historical figure, or a political stance (whatever is relevant to your domain) and then have the students write out what they think the character, user, figure, or person with that political belief would say, think, do, and feel.

37. Writing Prompts.

Have students generate 5 writing prompts that they would want to see on the final exam.

38. News Report.

Students create a news report and record a newscast discussion on a topic pertinent to instruction that week.

39. Dynamic Polling.

Use dynamic polling to assess understanding in real time.

40. Podcast.

Pair students up into teams of two and have them create a podcast discussing a recent textbook chapter or chapter of fiction they have been reading.

41. Create a Webliography.

Students create a webliography or collection of linked web-based resources on an assigned topic.

42. Wikipedia Entry.

Assign students a concept and have them create a Wikipedia entry for it. Let students know you will be running submissions through plagiarism software to make sure they haven't been copied.

43. Job Description or Want Ad.

Ask students what occupation they intend to pursue and have them research and write a job description or want ad for the occupation including what level of schooling you would have to attain to obtain a position in the field as well as average salary and prevalence of open positions in your area.

44. Design an Experiment.

Students must design an online experiment including development of a questionnaire, research question, hypothesis, methods, etc. and write up a brief proposal on their study.

45. Letter to the Editor or Government Official.

Have students write a letter to the editor of the local paper or a government official on a topic of local concern.

46. Try Something New.

Students must try something new that they have never tried before and then present a persuasive oral report to the class either encouraging other students to try it or warning students not to try it.

47. Electronic Portfolio.

Have students create an electronic portfolio of their work for the year and submit it as their final exam.

48. Welcome to My TED Talk.

Have students reflect on their life thus far and think about what they can share that would be of value to others. Have them view several TED Talks and then develop their own Talk to be recorded and presented in class. Instructors can require that relevant course concepts be interwoven into the Talk depending on the subject matter.

49. Case Study.

Give students a list of historical figures undercredited in their field and ask them to research and provide an oral report case study to educate the class on how this person impacted their field and why they may not have received the credit they deserved. (EXAMPLES (Science): Rosalind Franklin, Lise Meitner, Alfred Russel Wallace, Chien-Shiung Wu, Alice Augusta Ball, Mary Anning, Charles Drew).

50. Group Problem Solving.

Provide a case and have students propose a solution they work on together.

51. Concept Library.

Have students identify the concepts they are struggling with. Then have them find online resources that were helpful toward explaining the concept and create a concept library of information.

52. Idea "Speed Dating".

Students cycle through online breakouts rooms. They have five minutes to present their ideas to multiple audiences.

53. Chain Storytelling.

In the discussion forum, create a brief prompt or scenario to start the story. Then each student must reply with a continuation of the story by adding 3 sentences to it to create one cohesive story.

54. Glossary.

Create a web-based glossary with links to definitions or examples for words provided by the instructor.

55. Children's Book.

Students write and illustrate a children's book on a person or concept that demonstrates their knowledge.

56. Virtual Science Lab Interactives.

Students must engage in a lab simulation and write up lab notes or a brief report on the outcome.

    a. https://www.explorelearning.com/
    b. https://www.pbs.org/wgbh/nova/labs/lab/evolution/
    c. https://learn.concord.org/
    d. https://www.youngscientistlab.com/teachers/interactives
    e. https://www.inqits.com/

57. Itinerary.

Students create an itinerary for a trip to a different country including where they will stay, how they will get there, what activities they will engage in, a budget, and where they will eat. They must provide links to activities and create a presentation with photos and/or video.

58. Comic Strip.

Students must draw a comic strip to demonstrate their understanding of a historical event, fictional event, or scientific concept (whatever is relevant to the domain).

59. Talk Show Interview.

Pair students up. One student will pretend to be an important historical figure or fictional character and the other student will interview them.

60. Linked In Profile.

Students create a Linked In profile for a relevant historical figure, fictional character, or for their future selves.

5

TOOLS

In this chapter I provide a list of tools that can be used in the online courseroom by teachers to create content, deliver instruction, and provide feedback and by students to complete assignments and projects, refine writing, seek out additional resources, and communicate. This list is by no means comprehensive. It is intended to make you aware of the many tools available and to be a jumping off point with links to help you research tools that could be used in your online classes to enhance learning and engagement and take full advantage of the digital platform. Some of these tools pull double duty so you may find them under more than one category.

Annotation

Annotation tools can be used to analyze digital texts collaboratively. It can be used in many different ways including collaborative creation of materials, enhancement of documents, providing feedback, and annotating for learning and analysis.

Hypothesis https://web.hypothes.is/

NowComment https://nowcomment.com/

Concept Maps

Concept maps or mind mapping software is often used as a brainstorming tool to boost the writing process or to communicate ideas in a visual format.

BrainSharper https://brain-sharper.com/

Canva https://www.canva.com/

CmapTools https://cmap.ihmc.us/

Lucidchart https://www.lucidchart.com/pages/

MindMapper https://www.mindmanager.com/en/

Mindomo https://www.mindomo.com/

XMind https://www.xmind.net/

Conferencing

Videoconferencing is a valuable two-way communication tool. It can be used for many purposes including delivering synchronous lectures, recording lectures for asynchronous delivery, collaboration on group projects, meetings, and office hours.

*Black Board https://www.blackboard.com/teaching-learning/learning-management

*Canvas https://www.instructure.com/canvas

Skype https://www.skype.com/en/

Zoom https://www.zoom.us/

* These Learning Management System's have their own built-in videoconferencing.

Content

There are countless educational sites on the internet that can be useful supplemental tools in the online classroom. The content can be used in a multitude of ways including as a jumping off point or introduction to a topic for discussions, as a resource, or as another mode of delivery to increase student engagement and interest.

Academic Earth https://academicearth.org/

Alison https://alison.com/

Big Think https://bigthink.com/

Boss Club https://www.bossclub.com

Coursera https://www.coursera.org/

Cudoo https://cudoo.com

GoSkills https://www.goskills.com/

EdX https://www.edx.org/

Flocabulary https://www.flocabulary.com/

Kahn Academy https://www.khanacademy.org/

Lesson Planet https://www.lessonplanet.com

Master Class www.masterclass.com

TedX https://www.ted.com/

Think Tank Scholar https://www.thinktankscholar.com

Udemy https://www.udemy.com/

YouTube https://www.youtube.com/

Content Creation Tools

The tools listed below may be used by instructors to create assignments or by students to complete assigned projects. Some of the tools below can be deployed to create word or math crossword puzzles, flash cards, quiz games, word searches, comic books, storybooks, interactive graphs, bingo games, and much more.

Adobe Spark https://spark.adobe.com/

Book Creator https://bookcreator.com/

BookWidgets https://www.bookwidgets.com/

Comic Life http://plasq.com/apps/comiclife/macwin/

Kahoot! https://kahoot.com/

Padlet https://padlet.com/

Storybird https://storybird.com/

Tellagami https://tellagami.com/

Venngage https://venngage.com

Language Editors

This category of tool provides spelling, style, and grammar checking, identifying errors to help students proof their work before submission.

After the Deadline https://www.afterthedeadline.com/

AutoCrit https://www.autocrit.com/

Ginger www.gingersoftware.com

GrammarChecker https://www.grammarcheck.net/editor/

Grammarly https://www.grammarly.com/

Hemmingway Editor https://hemingwayapp.com/

PaperRater https://www.paperrater.com/

ProWritingAid https://prowritingaid.com/

Learning Management Systems

Learning Management Systems are generally web-based platforms that contain the elements necessary to teach a fully online course including instructional deliverables like lectures, videos, audio recordings, readings, video-conferencing, and multi-media as well as assessment capacity, messaging, and gradebook.

Black Board https://www.blackboard.com/teaching-learning/learning-management

Brightspace https://www.d2l.com/higher-education/products/core/

Canvas https://www.instructure.com/canvas

Edmodo https://new.edmodo.com/

Google Classroom https://edu.google.com/products/classroom/

Moodle https://moodle.org/

Sakai https://www.sakailms.org/

Plagiarism Detection Tools

Plagiarism detection tools use artificial intelligence to compare submitted work with a massive corpus of content to determine if it is original. Most tools provide an originality percentage that instructors can use to evaluate whether plagiarism has occurred. As most institutions have policies related to academic integrity, plagiarism detection is a valuable tool to document instances of cheating.

Copyleaks https://copyleaks.com/

Dublichecker https://www.duplichecker.com/

Grammarly https://www.grammarly.com/

Plagiarism Detector https://plagiarismdetector.net/

Turnitin https://www.turnitin.com/

Polling

Polling tools can be used synchronously to gauge understanding for real time formative assessment and instant feedback.

EZ-VOTE Connect https://info.gartnerdigitalmarkets.com/meridia-interactive-solutions-gdm-lp?category=Polling&utm_source=capterra

Flisti https://flisti.com/

Micropoll http://www.micropoll.com/

Mentimeter https://www.mentimeter.com/

Poll Everywhere https://www.polleverywhere.com/

Presentations

Software that streamlines the design elements of presentations can be used by both student and teacher to present information to the class. It is a learning tool that is useful both in the online classroom as well as in the workplace as many careers require visually supplemented verbal communication skills.

Flipgrid https://info.flipgrid.com/

Google Slides https://www.google.com/slides/about/

Padlet https://padlet.com/

PowerPoint https://www.microsoft.com/en-us/microsoft-365/powerpoint

Powtoon https://www.powtoon.com/

Proctoring

Proctoring software is used to ensure the integrity of exams. These tools can be used to verify the identity of the individual taking the exam and flag suspicious activity that could connote cheating such as looking at notes, requesting help from others, or browsing websites or mobile devices to find the answers to the exam questions. Some companies even provide live proctors.

AI Proctor https://www.aiproctor.com/artificial-intelligence

Examity https://www.examity.com/

ExamSoft https://examsoft.com/

Examus https://examus.com/

Proctor Exams https://proctorexams.com/

ProctorFree https://proctorfree.com/

ProctorU https://www.proctoru.com/services/software-proctoring

Speech-to-Text and Text-to-Speech Tools

Speech-to-text tools can be used by instructors to record feedback or by students to write notes or papers. Speech-to-text can also be invaluable to students with visual and learning disabilities. Text-to-speech tools can be used by students to proof and facilitate editing of their papers before they submit them for grading. When students read their papers to themselves, they often miss grammatical and spelling errors. I regularly advise students to at least listen to their paper read aloud by a software program so that they can hear any issues and make the proper revisions prior to submission.

Apple Dictation https://www.apple.com/accessibility/

Dragon https://www.dragon-naturally-speaking.com/

Speechnotes https://speechnotes.co/

Windows Dictation https://www.windowscentral.com/how-use-voice-dictationwindows-10

Streaming Video

Media tools such as the ones listed below allow users to create and host videos and allow for sharing. These tools can also be used to provide a vehicle for comment, data collection, tracking, and captioning.

Brightcove https://www.brightcove.com/en/

Dacast https://www.dacast.com/

GoToMeeting https://www.GoToMeeting.com/

Kaltura https://corp.kaltura.com/

Muvi https://www.muvi.com/

Screencastomatic https://screencast-o-matic.com/

Wowza https://www.wowza.com/

Youtube https://www.youtube.com/

Survey

Online survey tools facilitate the collection of data and information that can be used in a multitude of ways including for research, formative feedback about the course itself, and to collect information about the backgrounds and prior experiences of students to customize the course to better meet their needs.

Alchemer https://www.alchemer.com/

Feedier https://feedier.com/

Google Forms https://www.google.com/forms/about/

LimeSurvey https://www.limesurvey.org/

Qualtrics https://www.qualtrics.com/

Survey Anyplace https://surveyanyplace.com/

Survey Legend https://www.surveylegend.com/

Survey Monkey https://www.surveymonkey.com/

6

ACCESSIBILITY - UNIVERSAL DESIGN

Universal Design for Learning (UDL) is a concept that involves designing and planning curriculum to address and satisfy the needs of all learners. The three main principles of UDL are that development of curriculum should incorporate multiple means of representation, expression, and engagement. Thus, learners should be provided with multiple ways of obtaining information, multiple ways to demonstrate what they have learned, and multiple ways of engaging them in the learning process by making content relevant, challenging, and interesting (Orkwis & McKlane, 1998).

UDL is a concept that should be incorporated into both f2f and online classrooms. However, online instructional delivery is particularly suited to UDL because there are less temporal or physical barriers which can impede provision of multiple paths to learning as there are in the f2f classroom. UDL is all about reducing barriers to learning for all students. This includes things such as simplifying instructions and repeating instructions,

Here is a bulleted list of UDL considerations that can be relatively easily incorporated into the online courseroom.

Multiple Ways of Delivering Information

- Lectures can be automatically captioned in Kaltura, YouTube, or other platforms to make content more accessible for students with learning disabilities, second language learners, or students with hearing impairments.
- Foundational content can be offered in multiple ways (e.g.

readings, textbooks, lectures, videos, audio, simulations etc.) in an online class to appeal to as many students as possible.

- Supplemental media to reinforce complex concepts can easily be provided via links to curated content.
- Learning objectives can be made easily available within each module so students can refer back to them throughout lessons.
- Text-to-speech tools can be used to read digital content aloud to students with vision impairments or dyslexia.
- Digital announcements can be used to remind students of due dates and other important information for students with executive dysfunction (e.g. ADHD).
- Providing all instructions in writing is essential for students with learning disabilities and second language learners so they can go back and re-read them.

Multiple Ways for Students to Demonstrate Learning

- Learning should be assessed in multiple ways including quizzes, discussions, assignments, papers, projects, portfolios, exams, etc.
- Chats and discussion forums allow students with hearing impairments to participate in active discussions.
- Online exams and quizzes can be graded instantly and provide immediate feedback.
- Recorded presentations and video assignments give students the opportunity to demonstrate and practice their verbal skills. Recording and editing video of themselves is a useful real-world skill.

Multiple Ways to Engage the Learner

- Recorded content can be sped up or slowed down to accommodate different paces of learning.
- Flexibility in workspace can be an advantage in online

courses. Students learning online can create the environment that works best for them if they are able. Some may need to study with headphones to block out distractions. This would be more difficult to achieve in a f2f classroom. Of course, not all students have this luxury and that should be taken into consideration.

- Digital content allows students to adjust the size and brightness for those with vision impairments.

- Content such as discussion prompts and assignments can more easily be changed on the fly to engage students in current events. For example, as mentioned previously, in April of 2020 I changed one of my discussion prompts in a Human Development course I was teaching to give students the opportunity to discuss the COVID-19 pandemic.

- Discussions in online forums require all students to participate which is impossible to achieve in most f2f classrooms. Students must also engage with at least one peer. This leads to higher levels of engagement with the material and satisfaction with the class.

Universal Design Resources

Burgstahler, S., & Cory, R. (2008). *Universal Design in Higher Education: From Principles to Practice.* Cambridge, MA: Harvard Education Press.

Hall. T. E., Meyer, A., & Rose, D. H. (2012). *Universal Design for Learning in the Classroom: Practical Applications (What Works for Special-Needs Learners).* The Guilford Press.

Kyei-Blankson, L., Blankson, J., & Ntuli, E. (2019). *Care and Culturally Responsive Pedagogy in Online Settings.* Information Science Reference.

Orkwis, R. & McLane, K. (1998). *A Curriculum Every Student Can Use: Design Principles for Student Access.* ERIC/OSEP Special Project.

Ralabate, P. K. (2016). *Your UDL Lesson Planner: The Step-by-Step Guide for Teaching all Learners.* Brookes Publishing.

Ralabate, P. K. & Nelso, L. L. (2017). *Culturally Responsive Design for English Learners: The UDL Approach.* CAST Professional Publishing.

Rapp, W.H. (2014). *Universal Design for Learning in Action: 100 Ways to Teach All Learners.* Brookes Publishing.

Rose, D. H. & Meyer, A. with Strangman, N. & Rappolt, G. (2002). *Teaching Every Student in the Digital Age: Universal Design for Learning.* Association for Supervision and Curriculum Development.

Rose, D. H., Meyer, A. & Hitchcock, C. (2005). *The Universally Designed Classroom: Accessible Curriculum and Digital Technologies.* Harvard Education Press

Rose, D. H. & Meyer, A. (2006). *A Practical Reader in Universal Design for Learning.* CAST Professional Publishing.

Silvia, P. (2018). *Disability and Accessibility in the Virtual Classroom: Practical Tips for Designing Human-Friendly Online Courses.*

Schelly, C. L., Davies, P. L., & Spooner, C. L. (2011). Student Perceptions of Faculty Implementation of Universal Design for Learning. *Journal of Postsecondary Education and Disability, 24*(1), 17-28.

7

SUPPORT - RESEARCH

In this chapter I will provide a brief bibliographical review of some of the research literature pertaining to online learning. For those of you who have previous long-term online teaching experience, the efficacy of it may be evident. I wanted to provide this chapter to address those who may be more skeptical about online learning, especially those who were thrown into the deep end against their wishes. Learning curves are always uncomfortable under the best of circumstances. What many of you had to endure may have influenced your perceptions of the potential of online learning. This literature review will hopefully assure you that quality online learning can be just as effective as f2f learning and may even offer some unique advantages.

Anderson, T & Elloumi, F. (2004). *Theory and Practice of Online Learning.*

This book is a collection of chapters (16 in all) that reflects on more than 150 years of distance learning. Topics covered include: Foundations of Educational Theory for Online Learning, The Development of Online Courses, and Supporting the Online Learner. Chapters focus on pedagogy, course development, and theory. Each author is an experienced distance learning instructor and practitioner.

Bangert, A. W. (2004) The Seven Principles of Good Practice: a framework for evaluating on-line teaching. *Internet and Higher Education*, 7, 217–232. doi: 10.1016/j.iheduc.2004.06.003.

The Seven Principals of Good Practice were used as the basis to develop a 35-item questionnaire. The questionnaire was then given to 24 graduate level students in an educational statistics course. The questionnaire was written to evaluate whether evidence-based components of quality instruction were present in this online statistics course. Factors assessed included: student-faculty contact, cooperation among students, active learning, prompt feedback, time on task, high expectations, and diverse ways of learning. Results revealed that students in the course were highly satisfied with the course (92%). High levels of satisfaction were evident for all factors evaluated. Students did express that an introduction to the technology and instructor at the top of the class would have been helpful and made for an easier transition to the online format.

Bernard, R. M., Abrami, P. C., Lou, Y., Borokhovski, E., Wade, A., Wozney, L., Wallet, P. A. Fiset, M., Huang., B. (2004). How does distance education compare to classroom instruction? A Meta-analysis of Empirical Literature. *Review of Educational Research*, 74(3), 379–439.

A meta-analysis compared synchronous online and asynchronous online instruction with f2f instruction. The authors found that the asynchronous online students outperformed students in f2f classrooms. However, f2f students were found to outperform students in the synchronous online sections.

Bolliger, D. U. & Martin, F. (2018). Instructor and student perceptions of online student engagement strategies, *Distance Education*, 39(4), 568–583.

Student engagement is related to persistence, satisfaction, and performance. This study was undertaken to determine if there is agreement among instructors and students regarding the effectiveness of engagement strategies for online courses. A total of 161 online instructors and 155 online students responded to a survey on the subject. Learner-learner, learner-instructor, and learner-content were all found to be important to student engagement from both the student and teacher perspective.

Caton, J. B., Chung, S., Adeniji, N., Hom, J., Brar, K., Gallant, A., Bryant, M., Hain, A., Basaviah, P., & Hosamani, P. (2021). Student engagement in the online classroom: Comparing preclinical medical student question-asking behaviors in a videoconference versus in-person learning environment. *FASEBBioAdvances, 3*(2), 110-117.

This study was conducted following the COVID-19 pandemic when educational programs were forced to quickly convert their curricula to online delivery. The researchers wanted to determine if there were differences in levels of engagement following the switch to a large-group synchronous online delivery method for their preclinical Practice of Medicine program. They measured the differences in question-asking behaviors between previous in-person courses relative to online. Results revealed that instructors answered more questions and spent more time answering questions in the online sessions relative to the in-person sessions. Questions were also evaluated for complexity and it was found that more questions of higher complexity were asked in the online sessions versus the f2f sessions.

Driscoll, A., Jicha, K., Hunt, A. N., Tichavsky, L., and Thompson, G. (2012). Can online courses deliver in-class results? A comparison of student performance and satisfaction in an online versus a face-to-face introductory sociology course. *American Sociological Association, 40*, 312–313. doi: 10.1177/0092055X12446624

Driscoll, et. al. conducted a study of 368 sociology students in online and f2f courses taught by the same instructor for both methods. Student performance and satisfaction were compared to determine whether there were any differences related to modality. Results revealed that there were no differences in performance or satisfaction level between the two groups suggesting that online learning was just as effective as f2f learning in this study.

Gupta, M. M., Jankie, S., Pancholi, S. S., Talukdar, D., Sahu, P. K., & Sa, B. (2020). Asynchronous environment assessment: A pertinent option for medical and allied health profession education during the COVID-19 pandemic. *Education Sciences, 10*(12), 1-15.

The researchers wished to investigate whether the principles of, "integrity, equity, inclusiveness, fairness, ethics, and safety" could be achieved in asynchronous instruction during the COVID-19 pandemic. The authors suggest that open-ended short answer questions, oral exams, recorded exams, and problem-based questions that require application of knowledge are the best fit for asynchronous courses. They also advocated for surveillance during text taking to insure the validity of the exam.

Hurlbut, A. R. (2018). Online vs. traditional learning in teacher education: a comparison of student progress. *The American Journal of distance Education,* 32 (4), 248-266.

This study looked at what factors tend to influence performance. Performance measures consisted of student grades on assignments, questionnaires, and participation. The strength of this design was that the same instructor taught both the in-person and the online versions of the section so the instructor could be held constant, and the focus would be on the method rather than who delivered the content. Analysis of student's grades found that the online format was effective, and analysis of the satisfaction questionnaires reveled that students in both sections were equally satisfied with the course. The researchers found that student preference was important. Students who were more comfortable in online courses tended to perform better in the online format relative to those students who were not comfortable with the online format. Regardless of format, students indicated that instructor presence, interaction, and feedback were the most important elements and most crucial to their success.

Means, B., Toyama, Y., Murphy, R., & Baki, M. (2013). The effectiveness of online and blended learning: A meta-analysis of the empirical literature. *Teachers College Record,* 115(3), 1-47.

This meta-analysis was conducted to evaluate the efficacy of online and hybrid (blended) courses vs. f2f instruction across 45 different studies. The studies covered in the meta-analysis were both fully randomized experiments or quasi-experiments. Effect sizes were compared to determine the differences between the groups. The meta-analysis revealed that students in the online conditions performed slightly better than those in the f2f condition. The bulk of the effect was found in the comparison between the hybrid courses and the f2f courses. Authors suggest that the additional learning time, resources, and elements of the online courses may have been differentiating factors.

Pei, L. & Wu, H. (2019) Does online learning work better than offline learning in undergraduate medical education? A systematic review and meta-analysis. *Medical Education Online*, 24 (1), doi: 10.1080/10872981.

The authors conducted a meta-analysis accessing a 17-year period from 2000 to 2017 of studies investigating the knowledge level and skills of undergraduate medical students. The meta-analysis included 16 studies. Results showed that there were no statistically significant differences in skills and knowledge when comparing online and f2f students.

Paul, J. & Jefferson, F. (2019). A comparative analysis of student performance in an online vs. face-to-face environmental science course from 2009 to 2016, *Frontiers in Computer Science*, 1, 1-9.

A comparative analysis was conducted comparing online vs. f2f learning in an Environmental Science course over an eight-year period from 2009 to 2016. Growth in student performance was compared across modalities to determine whether one method was more effective than the other. Statistical analysis revealed no significant differences between performance for f2f students relative to online students overall. The study also investigated whether gender or class rank would influence the results. There were no significant differences based on gender or class rank, as well.

Rovai, A. P., & Barnum, K. T. (2003). On-Line course effectiveness: An analysis of student interactions and perceptions of learning. *Journal of Distance Learning*, 18(1), 57-73.

In this study the researchers were interested in student perceptions of online learning across 19 graduate level courses. The authors found that female students were much more satisfied and reported greater online learning relative to their male counterparts. They believe this might be related to gendered differences in communication style. The main finding overall was that students who were more involved in classroom discussions were also more likely to be satisfied with the class, suggesting that providing students with ways to interact with each other and the instructor should be a requirement in online course construction. Results of the study also revealed a great deal of variability across courses, suggesting that instructional design decisions and quality control may be important to focus on when developing curriculum for online classes. This finding prompted the authors to suggest that interpretation on the efficacy of online teaching should be tempered by the fact that there are many confounds including pedagogy, technology, and the students themselves that may hinder accurate interpretation of this literature.

Richardson, J. C., & Swan, K. (2003). Examining social presence in online courses in relation to students' perceived learning and satisfaction. *Journal of Asynchronous Learning Networks, 7*(1), 68-88.

A correlational design was employed, and 97 students participated in this study of student perceived learning and satisfaction with online courses. Students who perceived high levels of social presence also scored high on perceived learning and satisfaction with the instructor. Thus, instructor responsivity to questions and communications as well as opportunities to engage with their peers and instructor was related to whether students felt that they had a positive learning experience.

Verduin, J.R., & Clark, T.A. (1991). *Distance Education: The Foundations of Effective Practice.* San Francisco, CA: Jossey-Bass.

The authors reviewed 56 studies and found that online education was equivalent to or better than learning in traditional courses on a range of outcomes and perceptions. As with most things, how the technology was deployed appeared to have more of an impact on effectiveness than the method. They suggested that distance learning can be as effective as f2f instruction if there is good alignment between the technology and the instructional task, there is a good amount of student-student interaction, and there is timely and comprehensive feedback from instructors.

Weschke, B., Barclay, R. D., & Vandersall, K. (2011). Online teacher education: Exploring the impact of a reading and literacy program on student learning. *Journal of Asynchronous Learning Network,* 15(2), 22-43.

Researchers studied the impact of teachers who completed a fully online teacher training program in elementary level reading pedagogy and content-specialization. There were 70 teachers in the study and observations for nearly 4,000 student observations over a three-year period were analyzed. A significant positive effect was found, meaning that students of teachers in the online program increased student learning just as much as or more than students who were taught in a traditional teacher education program.

SUPPORT - RESEARCH

Anderson, T & Elloumi, F. (2004). *Theory and Practice of Online Learning.*

Bangert, A. W. (2004) The Seven Principles of Good Practice: a framework for evaluating on-line teaching. *Internet and Higher Education*, 7, 217–232. doi: 10.1016/j.iheduc.2004.06.003.

Bernard, R. M., Abrami, P. C., Lou, Y., Borokhovski, E., Wade, A., Wozney, L., Wallet, P. A. Fiset, M., Huang., B. (2004). How does distance education compare to classroom instruction? A Meta-analysis of Empirical Literature. *Review of Educational Research*, 74(3), 379–439.

Bolliger, D. U. & Martin, F. (2018) Instructor and student perceptions of online student engagement strategies, *Distance Education*, vol. 39, no. 4, pp. 568–583. doi: 10.1080/01587919.2018.1520041

Burgstahler, S., & Cory, R. (2008). *Universal Design in Higher Education: From Principles to Practice.* Cambridge, MA: Harvard Education Press.

Caton, J. B., Chung, S., Adeniji, N., Hom, J., Brar, K., Gallant, A., Bryant, M., Hain, A., Basaviah, P., & Hosamani, P. (2021). Student engagement in the online classroom: Comparing preclinical medical student question-asking behaviors in a videoconference versus in-person learning environment. *FASEBBioAdvances, 3(2), 110-117.*

Driscoll, A., Jicha, K., Hunt, A. N., Tichavsky, L., and Thompson, G. (2012). Can online courses deliver in-class results? A comparison of student performance and satisfaction in an online versus a face-to-face introductory sociology course. *American Sociological Association,* 40, 312–313. doi: 10.1177/0092055X12446624

Gupta, M. M., Jankie, S., Pancholi, S. S., Talukdar, D., Sahu, P. K., & Sa, B. (2020). Asynchronous environment assessment: A pertinent option for medical and allied health profession education during the COVID-19 pandemic. *Education Sciences,* 10 (12), 1-15.

Hall. T. E., Meyer, A., & Rose, D. H. (2012). *Universal Design for Learning in the Classroom: Practical Applications (What Works for Special-Needs Learners).* The Guilford Press.

Hurlbut, A. R. (2018). Online vs. traditional learning in teacher education: a comparison of student progress. *The American Journal of distance Education,* 32(4), 248-266.

Kyei-Blankson, L., Blankson, J., & Ntuli, E. (2019). *Care and Culturally Responsive Pedagogy in Online Settings.* Information Science Reference.

Karl, K. A., O'Leary-Kelly, A. M., & Martocchio, J. J. (1993). The impact of feedback and self-efficacy on performance in training. *Journal of Organizational Behavior,* 14(4), 379-394.

Means, B., Toyama, Y., Murphy, R., & Baki, M. (2013). The effectiveness of online and blended learning: A meta-analysis of the empirical literature, *Teachers College Record,* 115(3), 1-47.

Orkwis, R. & McLane, K. (1998). *A Curriculum Every Student Can Use: Design Principles for Student Access.* ERIC/OSEP Special Project.

Pei, L. & Wu, H. (2019) Does online learning work better than offline learning in undergraduate medical education? A systematic review and meta-analysis. *Medical Education Online,* 24 (1), doi: 10.1080/10872981.

Paul, J. & Jefferson, F. (2019). A comparative analysis of student performance in an online vs. face-to-face environmental science course from 2009 to 2016, *Frontiers in Computer Science,* 1, 1-9.

Ralabate, P. K. (2016). *Your UDL Lesson Planner: The Step-by-Step Guide for Teaching all Learners.* Brookes Publishing.

Ralabate, P. K. & Nelso, L. L. (2017). *Culturally Responsive Design for English Learners: The UDL Approach.* CAST Professional Publishing.

Rapp, W.H. (2014). *Universal Design for Learning in Action: 100 Ways to Teach All Learners.* Brookes Publishing.

Richardson, J. C., & Swan, K. (2003). Examining social presence in online courses in relation to students' perceived learning and satisfaction. *Journal of Asynchronous Learning Networks, 7*(1), 68-88.

Rose, D. H. & Meyer, A. with Strangman, N. & Rappolt, G. (2002). *Teaching Every Student in the Digital Age: Universal Design for Learning.* Association for Supervision and Curriculum Development.

Rose, D. H., Meyer, A. & Hitchcock, C. (2005). *The Universally Designed Classroom: Accessible Curriculum and Digital Technologies.* Harvard Education Press

Rose, D. H. & Meyer, A. (2006). *A Practical Reader in Universal Design for Learning.* CAST Professional Publishing.

Rovai, A. P., & Barnum, K. T. (2003). On-Line course effectiveness: An analysis of student interactions and perceptions of learning. *Journal of Distance Learning, 18*(1), 57-73.

Roy, R., Potter, S., Yarrow, K., & Smith, M., (2005*). Towards Sustainable Higher Education: Environmental impacts of campus-based and distance higher education systems.* Final Report March, 2005. http://www3.open. ac.uk/events/3/2005331_47403_01.pdf

Silvia, P. (2018). *Disability and Accessibility in the Virtual Classroom: Practical Tips for Designing Human-Friendly Online Courses.*

Schelly, C. L., Davies, P. L., & Spooner, C. L. (2011). Student Perceptions of Faculty Implementation of Universal Design for Learning. *Journal of Postsecondary Education and Disability, 24*(1), 17-28.

Verduin, J.R., & Clark, T.A. (1991). *Distance education: The foundations of effective practice.* San Francisco, CA: Jossey-Bass.

Weschke, B., Barclay, R. D., & Vandersall, K. (2011). Online teacher education: Exploring the impact of a reading and literacy program on student learning. Journal of Asynchronous Learning Network, 15(2), 22-43.

APPENDIX

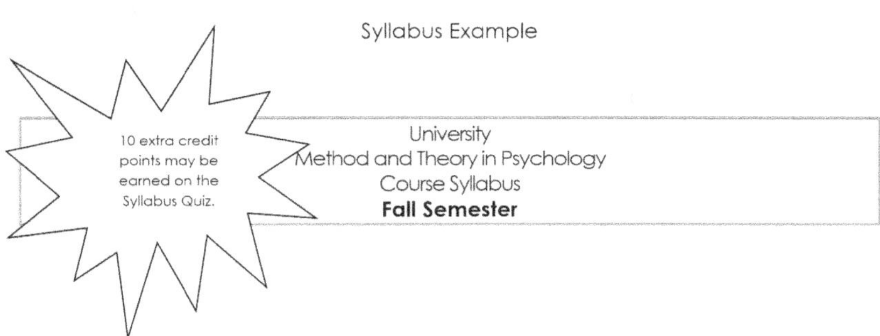

Professor:

e-mail:

Office Phone:

"Office" hours:

Course Description and Objectives:

This course provides an introduction to research methods and theory in the field of psychology. Research methods allow psychologists to describe, predict, explain, and determine causes of behavior. In addition, an understanding of research methods is essential for becoming a critical consumer of research.

The following topics will be emphasized: the role of scientific inquiry in psychology, research questions, ethics in research, <u>writing</u> in psychology, reliability, validity, and research designs.

General Education Objectives for the Physical and Life Sciences (PLS):

-Demonstrate a broad understanding of scientific principles and the ways scientists in particular disciplines conduct research.

-Solve complex problems requiring the application of scientific concepts.

-Examine the scientific basis of complex questions, including how science impacts political, social, economic, or ethical issues.

-Critically evaluate scientific arguments and understand the limits of scientific knowledge.

-Communicate scientific ideas clearly and effectively.

Course Objectives:

-Understand, apply, and engage in scholarly writing about basic research methods in psychology.

-Demonstrate understanding of the different research methods used by psychologists.

-Evaluate the appropriateness of conclusions derived from research and media.

-Choose research designs that are appropriate to study questions.

-Develop academic and scholarly writing skills.

Upon completion of the course, you should possess an understanding of the fundamental principles and procedures of psychological research and be capable of producing polished academic written reports using APA Style.

Required Texts:

1) Cozby, P. C. & Bates, P. *Methods in Behavioral Research*, 13th Ed. New York: McGraw Hill.

Textbook is available in the bookstore and on the web.

2) *American Psychological Association Publication Manual* (6th or 7th edition). Washington D.C.: American Psychological Association.

Available at Amazon.com or BarnesandNoble.com for sale or rent.

General Course Requirements

All quizzes, assignments, and the discussion forums will be open on the first day of class and you can complete them any time before the deadline if you want to move ahead. However, you must complete them BY the deadline as they will each close on the dates indicated in the table. The Midterm and Final Exam are the only tasks that must be completed on the assigned dates. A 24 hour window will be opened and the exams can be completed on those dates only. The Psych Department requires that you complete 2 hours of experimental credit. Make sure to do so before the end of the semester. You must also assign your credits to this class or they will not be visible to me on the website. More information can be found on the Info, Syllabus, and Subject Pool Requirement tab.

1) DISCUSSION PARTICIPATION: Every student will be expected to participate in online discussions. Students are expected to both a) respond to this question each week (by Wednesday of the assigned week) and b) respond to one classmate each week (by Sunday of the assigned week). 40 points are possible. A student who participates every week will receive the entire amount at the end of the term. Those who participate less will be given points proportional to their level of participation. Please exercise good judgment in your posts. Negative or abusive comments will not be tolerated. The forum should be used for rigorous yet civil discourse that is on topic.

The discussion forum will also contain an area for students to pose questions to the professor that the entire class might benefit from or be able to answer. If you have a question about the course or assignments, please look at the Course Questions forum first to see if the question has already been posed and answered. If you have the answer to a question posed by a classmate, please feel free to answer them. The professor will be reviewing this forum on a regular basis and will answer any unanswered questions. Emails should be reserved for any private or confidential communications with the professor.

2) CHAPTER QUIZZES: Brief, 10 item quizzes will be given throughout the course based upon the Cozby chapter assigned for that week. They will each be worth 10 points and provide you with ongoing feedback about your understanding of the chapter. You may use your book as a reference. You will be able to drop one quiz.

3) EXAMS: You will be evaluated on your understanding of the material by taking two exams. Each exam will include questions based on the readings, lectures, and discussion. The mid-term will include all content up until that point and the final will be comprehensive. No make-up exams will be given unless arrangements are made **prior** to an exam or proof of necessary absenteeism (e.g., a Dr. note). Exams will NOT be open-book and will be available for a fixed amount of time.

4) THE PSYCHOLOGY OF PROPAGANDA PAPER: It is an important objective of this class to provide you with the skills necessary to become an informed and critical consumer of information. Thus, you will be required to complete a 6-page APA Style academic think paper on the topic of The Psychology of Propaganda. Follow the detailed instructions to receive full credit.

5) RESEARCH PROPOSAL TOPICS AND REFERENCES: You will have the opportunity to turn in your proposed topic and references (at least 5!) for the research proposal paper to receive some initial feedback. This is worth 20 points.

6) RESEARCH PROPOSAL: In order to demonstrate your understanding of research and your writing skills, you will complete a research proposal. The paper must include a cover page, abstract, introduction, aims of your research project, method section, and references

section. The final research paper must be in APA style. There are examples of what each section should include in the APA Manual. You may also consult peer reviewed journals, though the APA Manual is the ultimate source since it will describe what an actual manuscript should look like. There will also be a sample paper on the website in the Writing Resources tab. The paper should be no more than 8 pages long (1 inch margins, 12-pt font, double spaced, not including the title page and reference page). Please consult the Writing Resources tab as it will contain everything you need to know to be successful on the paper including instructions, PowerPoint, rubric, and sample paper. Please keep in mind that this is a RESEARCH paper and thus requires a professional and technical voice (this kind of writing is very different from the writing you have been doing in literature courses, so keep that in mind).

	Points
Discussion Participation	40
Quizzes	70
Psych of Propaganda Paper	50
Research Proposal Topics and References	20
Research Proposal	100
Midterm Exam	50
Final Exam	50
Total Points	**380**

GRADING:

Grades will be computed as follows:
Letter grades:

A: 342-380 points
B: 304-341 points
C: 266-303 points
D: 228-265 points
F: 0 – 227 points

<u>Course Schedule</u>

* unless otherwise indicated, chapter readings refer to the Cozby Text

WEEK 1: Sept 1 to 6 **Introduction and Overview/ Scientific Understanding of Behavior**

Mon	Tue	Wed	Thurs	Fri	Sat	Sun
	First Day of Class			Intro Video Due		Syllabus quiz due

WEEK 2: Sept 7 to 13 **Scientific Understanding of Behavior (cont'd)**

Mon	Tue	Wed	Thurs	Fri	Sat	Sun
Ch 1		Discussion Question 1 Comment				Discussion Question 1 Reply Quiz 1

Mon	Tue	Wed	Thurs	Fri	Sat	Sun
Ch 2						

WEEK 3: Sept 14 to 20 **Science and Research Questions**

WEEK 4: Sept 21 to 27 **Searching the Literature**

Mon	Tue	Wed	Thurs	Fri	Sat	Sun
		Discussion Question 2 Comment				Discussion Question 2 Reply Quiz 2

WEEK 5: Sept 28 to Oct 4 **Ethics**

Mon	Tue	Wed	Thurs	Fri	Sat	Sun
Ch 3	Topics and References Due	Discussion Question 3 Comment				Discussion Question 3 Reply Quiz 3

WEEK 6: Oct 5 to 11 **Variables**

Mon	Tue	Wed	Thurs	Fri	Sat	Sun
Ch 4				Midterm Ch 1-4		

WEEK 7: Oct 12 to 18 **Writing in Psychology**

Mon	Tue	Wed	Thurs	Fri	Sat	Sun
APA Manual Appendix A and Ch 1-3 Bem Article		Discussion Question 4 Comment				Discussion Question 4 Reply

WEEK 8: Oct 19 to 25 **Critical Thinking**

Mon	Tue	Wed	Thurs	Fri	Sat	Sun
Hobbs and McGee Article		Discussion Question 5 Comment		Psychology of Propaganda Paper Due		Discussion Question 5 Reply

WEEK 9: Oct 26 to Nov 1 **Measurement and Descriptive Statistics**

Mon	Tue	Wed	Thurs	Fri	Sat	Sun
Ch 5 and 12						Quiz 4

WEEK 10: Nov 2 to 8 **Survey Research**

Mon	Tue	Wed	Thurs	Fri	Sat	Sun
Ch 7		Discussion Question 6 Comment				Discussion Question 6 Reply Quiz 5

WEEK 11: Nov 9 to 15 **Nonexperimental Designs (Observational Methods)**

Mon	Tue	Wed	Thurs	Fri	Sat	Sun
Ch 6						Quiz 6

WEEK 12: Nov 16 to 22 **Experimental Design**

Mon	Tue	Wed	Thurs	Fri	Sat	Sun
Ch 8		Discussion Question 7 Comment				Discussion Question 7 Reply Quiz 7

WEEK 13: Nov 23 to 29 **Thanksgiving Break**

Mon	Tue	Wed	Thurs	Fri	Sat	Sun
Relax and enjoy your time off!						

WEEK 14: Nov 30 to Dec 6 **Conducting Experiments**

Mon	Tue	Wed	Thurs	Fri	Sat	Sun
Ch 9 Rosenthal Article		Discussion Question 8 Comment				Discussion Question 8 Reply

WEEK 15: Dec 7 to Dec 13 **Other Research Designs and Generalizing Results**

Mon	Tue	Wed	Thurs	Fri	Sat	Sun
Ch 11 and 14		Research Paper Due				

WEEK 16: Dec 14 to 21 **Summary and Review**

Mon	Tue	Wed	Thurs	Fri	Sat	Sun
	Final Exam					

General Course Policies:

1) This class will be most rewarding for you if you are an active participant and view this experience as a collaborative enterprise. To this end, throughout the semester you are encouraged to communicate with your peers in the discussion forums and are expected to keep up with all readings and assignments. Note that

your professor is located in the Pacific Time Zone (PST), so please be aware of this when attempting to communicate with her. The discussion board is for academic purposes only and will be monitored. Students are expected to behave honorably and to be polite and respectful to their professor and fellow classmates. Please put in effort into your posts. You will only get out what you put in and effort is factored into whether all points are given on each post and reply.

2) Additional information about this class, and a copy of the syllabus is available on the course web page (Canvas). Being unaware of course requirements and expectations is not an excuse for failing to complete any of the assignments in this course.

3) PowerPoint slides with audio explanations are provided which will expand upon and highlight content in the readings. These "lectures" are designed to aid in your understanding of the assigned readings, focus you on the most important material, and offer an opportunity to further your understanding.

4) Late assignments will not be accepted, and no make-up exams will be given unless arrangements are made **prior** to an exam or proof of inability to complete work (e.g., a Dr. note) is provided. If you unexpectedly miss an exam due to exceptional circumstances (e.g., family emergency or sudden illness), it is your responsibility to contact the professor within 24 hours of the exam to discuss the possibility of a make-up exam. Any make-up exam is likely to differ from the exam the rest of the class takes and will typically be in essay format.

5) Academic dishonesty will NOT be tolerated. Academic dishonesty includes (but is not

limited to) cheating on exams and plagiarism. Students caught participating in academic dishonesty will receive a score of zero on the relevant assignment. In addition, instances of academic dishonesty will be referred to the Scholastic Conduct Committee. Sanctions for academic dishonesty range from failing an assignment to failing a course or expulsion from the University. For additional information about University policies concerning academic dishonesty refer to:

6) University welcomes students with disabilities into all of the University's educational programs. In order to receive consideration for reasonable accommodations, a student with a disability must contact the appropriate disability services office at the campus where you are officially enrolled, participate in an intake interview, and provide documentation:

If the documentation supports your request for reasonable accommodations, your campus's disability services office will provide you with a Letter of Accommodations.

For Technical Issues:

Contact the help desk at XXX-XXX-XXXX

Syllabus Quiz Example:

1. Which topic will NOT be covered in this course?

    a. Reliability
    b. Validity
    c. Ethics
    d. Data mining

2. Who are the authors of the primary text for this course?

    a. Cozby & Bates
    b. Mullen & Garcia
    c. Silva & Santos
    d. Johnson & Montgomery

3. How many chapter quizzes are scheduled?

    a. 8
    b. 7
    c. 6
    d. 5

4. What is the minimum number of references to include in your research proposal?

    a. 6
    b. 3
    c. 10
    d. 5

5. What is the extra credit assignment?

    a. Write a poem about research methods
    b. Spurious correlation assignment
    c. Build a monument to research methods
    d. Podcast assignment

6. Which is NOT a description included about the Research Proposal?

    a. No more than 8 pages
    b. There are examples of what each section should include in the APA Manual
    c. It is a RESEARCH proposal and requires a professional and technical voice
    d. Must use Times New Roman font

7. What is/are your professor's preferred mode(s) of communication?

    a. Mail
    b. Telepathy
    c. Phone
    d. Email or Text

8. Which section is not included in the Research Proposal?

    a. Method
    b. Results
    c. Abstract
    d. Cover page

9. What does the syllabus say about missed exams?

   a. No make-ups unless prior arrangements have been made.
   b. A make-up exam would likely be in essay form.
   c. Instructor must be contacted within 24 hours to arrange a make-up exam
   d. All of the above

10. In which time zone is your professor located?

   a. Eastern
   b. Central
   c. Mountain
   d. Pacific

9 798749 950519